Ken White speaks in swerve and thistle, thinks in hinges, muscles a touch of molasses into his syntax to flex the metronome. This is dazzle. These are necessary jostlings, tangled thick in coursing minutes, intercourses. Here, texture and reference are overlapped concerns, as artifice and blankness are both garmented and undressed: lovers, a beast, contemporary Los Angeles. We hunger for these racings—to be disguised, to be revealed, to jump leagues, to be in thrall.
  —Richard Siken

Ken White's *The Getty Fiend* lives in its vast world of stunning lyric objectivity. The poems peril through strong characters, their chivalry of scope, breath, might, and myth, all to touch down in The J. Paul Getty Museum, and rejoice in a dream-vision of medieval modernism ("a SkyMall classic"). I always look to White's poetry to close the gap between the ancient and the innovative; this is a mighty and brilliant second collection of poetry that holds its discontented marvel of grandeur at "kiss of air" distance, but bewitches with its arresting caress and craft.
  —Prageeta Sharma

The Getty Fiend's poems squall with incomparable implication: necessary and livid éclat through our embalmèd darkness, "dialed to high." Every spiral of beauty on earth is changed under such duress. And such close observation exceeds lexical and idiosyncratic gymnastics—this is no mere concordance of hips and thighs. If there is obscurity here, it is on the part of the reader. If our phantasms are condensed, we might thank Ken White for his cinematic mitigations.
  —Joan Naviyuk Kane

Like Jean Cocteau's *La Belle et La Bête*, the alchemy of this dark romance is equal parts fabric, flesh, fur, and art direction. Ken White is the same sort of sorcerer of menace and allure, but *The Getty Fiend* is situated in contemporary Los Angeles, and in trailing the city's specters—ecstasy, vengeance, and transformation—the poet takes surface streets. In language textured as distinctly as the dress of its heroes (belted, placketed, buckled, and triple-stitched), bare bodies too are fully accounted, philtrum to perineum. How far in does the docent escort lead? What's behind this exhibit? Through these cretonne drapes? What Opera, Doc? Somewhere to surpass oneself. Wear this. Yes. You're the one. We've waited for you.
  —Brian Blanchfield

the
GETTY
fiend

KEN WHITE

Introduction by
Michael du Plessis

The Getty Fiend
FIRST EDITION
2015 Les Figues NOS Book Contest, Editors' Pick.

Text and cover design by Les Figues Press.

ISBN 13: 978-1-934254-69-1
ISBN 10: 1-934254-69-X
Library of Congress Control Number: 2017948417

Les Figues Press thanks its subscribers for their support and readership.
Les Figues Press is a 501c3 organization. Donations are tax-deductible.

Les Figues would like to thank Peter Binkow and Johanna Blakley for their ongoing
support and generosity.

Thank you to each of the following individuals for assisting with the NOS contest: lê thi
diem thúy, Teresa Carmody, Coco Owen, Sean Pessin, Divya Victor, and Andrew Wessels.

In producing this book, special thanks to Sasha Burik, Michael du Plessis, Lezlie Mayers,
and Vanessa Place.

Images adapted from Williams, Lacy, Rountree, and Meier's *The Getty Fiend Design
Process*, The J. Paul Getty Trust, 1991.

Les Figues Press titles are available through:
Les Figues Press, http://www.lesfigues.com
Small Press Distribution, http://www.spdbooks.org

Post Office Box 7736
Los Angeles, CA 90007
info@lesfigues.com
www.lesfigues.com

Let us not take pride as if we had merely outgrown
a childish fear. Let us examine the matter
without bias. Let us beware of judging hastily
the monsters of old, in new disguises.

Guy Endore, *The Werewolf of Paris*

INTRODUCTION TO *THE GETTY FIEND*
BY MICHAEL DU PLESSIS

Ken White's *The Getty Fiend* invents, in its title, the one thing (or perhaps, in museum terms, the one "acquisition") that both Getty Museums have sorely lacked: a fiend. To the Opera its phantom, to Paris its werewolf, to the Notre Dame its hunchback, and now, to the Getty, its fiend. Were it for this contribution to museology and monstrosity alone, *The Getty Fiend* would be a *necessary* book.

Yet White's book is necessary not only for its title. It is, paradoxically, necessary also for its sheer luxury, for the luxuriant profusion of its excess— *The Getty Fiend* is an excessively witty and excessively beautiful invention. A Getty-area comedy of manners turns into a "medieval melodrama" (as White's subtitle marks its genre). Or is it the other way round? Various werewolves fuse into one "Beast" called Kveldulfur to haunt the Getty via a miniature verse epic, a mock epic that is not without melancholy. The necessity of *The Getty Fiend* is not the dourness of the gloomily inevitable and the glumly expected. Instead, White's book (impossible to pin down or "[pinion]" in its genres, "Behold *The Beast* pinioned," p. 13) offers its fortunate readers an over-abundance of wit, of melodrama overflowing into comedy, camp even, were "camp" not (in its current commonly used sense) a reductive category to control its excess. There are whiplashes of epigrammatic incisiveness and incision: the lines, "It's a Sky Mall classic. Hollywood Forever/all over Gower" (p. 14) sound like acid descriptions of the soon-to-be Garcetti Los Angeles. There are passages of intricate gorgeousness, where LA appears under the spell of White's language:

```
To the north, an unreadable postcard: HUGE WHITE LETTERS claim
hillbrow's de facto altar with inscrutable signifying idols.
Far ahead, scrim of haze, sepia and pink. Ocean's dim teal hem.
```
(p. 6)

Or:

> Rightly so there came verily by the holy telescope
> at roost over the spangled worm of Western
> Avenue in its sinuous gold-lit gossamers and lurid stoplights
> and brake lights and green lights and come-hither headlights
> the evening gown of the ball python, marigold and lavender. (p. 26)

Camp can hold both "the evening gown of the ball python, marigold and lavender," the "scrim" and "hem" and the "Sky Mall Classics" simultaneously and cumulatively in the same conflicted space.

(But we will have to return, shortly, to camp and its questions.)

At least three werewolf tales turn into an Oscar Wildean adventure of language, of imagination, of wit, in all and every sense of wit: canny—and uncanny—inventiveness, seductive cleverness and exquisiteness of form.

The excess of *The Getty Fiend* depends, in one of the text's many glorious contradictions, on exquisite formal precision. White's line breaks are precise and sharp as pleats and folds of haute couture: the following passage displays— and with what wit!—overlay of the sartorial and the poetic, the medieval and the contemporary:

> [Then he donned
> a mackintosh of red sendal,
> mayhap by YSL, mayhap
> by D&G, and bare a
> mantle upon his shoulder
> that was furred with
> marten or with mink—lined
> in the high and ridiculous
> Burberry plaid—he'd seen
> all grown and smoking hot
> smoking fucking hot
> Hermione Granger in the
> ad—and the leer knight
> said unto the blear knight:
> Sirlet, my stunned
> confection, do attend...] (p. 26)

The book's eye for detail cuts, to mix metaphors (for *The Getty Fiend* invites its readers to do so), sharp as a razor. An acid lucidity etches the beautifully funny description of the Getty:

> —on a looming motte rests white-gold Camelot in fossiled block.
> Banners snap in sea wind atop buttercream barbicans. Smooth
> serpentine bailey gleams above broad green moat of succulents.
> Lesser structures scatter the foliate hillside.
> Locked in chain, segments of the endless millipede. Ten lanes of

besiegers strangulate the hill, grind unpredictable stop-and-go patterns to baffle castle sentries, flash shields emblazoned with battle cry in perpetuity: Interstate California 405. (p. 7)

Once we have encountered such a marvel, will we ever ascend to the beige travertine of the Getty without White's words accompanying and echoing our ascent?

Restless in its inventiveness, for *The Getty Fiend*, a single "Fiend" is not enough. At the very least, three werewolves—Marie de France's 13th-century shapeshifter, Guy Endore's early 20th-century lycanthrope, and Kvedulfur, a wolfman of Norse legend—inspirit *The Getty Fiend*, with Kveldulfur lending his magnificently tolling and resonant name to the central character of White's text.[i] The Getty becomes a medieval keep, a stronghold of the Middle Ages and surely the spectacular historical melodramas of Cecil B. DeMille cannot be far off. After all, White's text intermittently assumes the language, layout and typeface of the screenplay, the quintessentially Los Angeles literary form. Wholly written as screenplay, printed in the bombastically earnest typeface and formatting that seem to be part and parcel of the form, the prologue primes us for cinema, for movies. Screen and play: the text reverts at times to this form before turning again into poetic astonishment—much like the werewolf's reversion to its true shape. But is that wolf or human? Is *The Getty Fiend* a screenplay masquerading as poetry or poetry assuming the shape of a screenplay?

The prologue swoops in one long panorama over Los Angeles: "EXT. HIGH ABOVE LOS ANGELES, <u>FALCON CAM</u> – CONTINUOUS" (noting on its way, hilariously, a shabbier peregrine, "POV from the tousled shoulders of a peregrine," p. 6). Such a flourish recalls many a CGI opening fanfare, yet salvaged from banality here by its linguistic and imaginative exuberance:

```
EXT. GETTY RESEARCH PAVILION - CONTINUOUS

FALCON CAM wheels past scholars' cells, veers down a hidden
curvilinear path, hovers at alcove, RAPS.

With audible CRACK, wall surface sheds stone chips. A narrow,
handle-less door swings inward on silent hinges. (p. 10)
```

Gothic, indeed, as befits a book called *The Getty Fiend*, where falcons open secret doors but slapstick, too, as in Mel Brooks' parody of Hitchcock where a would-be panoptical craning shot turns to bathos when it gets its all-too material comeuppance.

The Getty Fiend flirts enchantingly with preciosity and over-refinement, flirts, but never quite embraces. For it owes as much to Robert Bresson's *Lancelot du Lac* as it does to *Monty Python and The Holy Grail*, as much to Djuna Barnes as to *Spamalot*, to Thomas Malory as much as "Jabberwocky."

And to pile on paradoxes and metamorphoses, *The Getty Fiend*'s comic richness shimmers with sadness like shot silk. This is comedy that will break the heart. Any text that begins,

```
OVER BLACK:
RUSH OF WIND.
Faint symphony of CAR HORNS grows louder…
FADE IN:
EXT. HIGH ABOVE LOS ANGELES, FALCON CAM - CONTINUOUS (p. 6)
```

And ends, "blizzard/of light/hush/susurration/of slight/hush" (pp. 96-97), right before "FADE TO WHITE" (p. 97), knows its movies and its melodrama. For melodrama whispers, always, "too late." *The Getty Fiend* is untimely, wondrously and melancholically too late. Like comedy, melodrama turns on timing, albeit a different temporality.

Melodrama, as White shows so movingly, means holding back your tears until that penultimate moment just before the curtain falls, the houselights go up, the words "The End" appear on the screen or, mercilessly here, a simple "FADE TO WHITE." That we wish immediately to reread the text after such an ending, to read it back from an alert that is anything but a spoiler, must be the strongest of the multiple spells the book casts.

Melodrama is a mode of excess and here indeed *The Getty Fiend* makes good on its subtitle.[ii] Yet camp is a mode of excess that is not altogether (or perhaps not at all) distinguishable from melodrama. And here the Fiend of Camp I invoked earlier makes its comeback. Anything and everything in *The Getty Fiend* doubles, redoubles, becomes duplicitous, as shape-shifty as its titular fiend—we should bear in mind that the word "fiend" can designate Satan, the Adversary (*der Feind*), a monster, an addict ("dope fiend"), or a possessed and properly fanatical fan (a "movie fiend"). Names both in the text or in its immediate (exorbitant) orbit take on multiple meanings: Kveldulfur (whose name, it seems, means, in one of its senses, "evening wolf" [Baring-Gould, p. 43]). Bisclavret (whom Marie de France takes care to point out, is a particular Breton term for what the other vernaculars call "garwalf" [quoted in Baring-Gould, p. 60]), or the Parisian werewolf are all masks, metonyms, metaphors for a young 21st-century Getty scholar.[iii] And the other way round too: a wolf in haute couture? Or a dandy in faux wolf fur?

And it is here, dear reader, that Susan Sontag makes her special cameo appearance. Her essay from 1964, "Notes on 'Camp'" (note the frisson, the thrill, of the "scare quotes") has become so canonized that we may miss its many ambiguities about ambiguities. Sontag offers 58 notes on camp.[iv] (Yes, Sontag does number the notes, whether for campiness or not.) Note 16 remarks:

> Thus, the Camp sensibility is one that is alive to a double sense in which some things can be taken. But this is not that familiar split-level construction of a literal meaning, on the one hand, and a symbolic meaning, on the other. It is the difference, rather, between the thing as meaning something, anything, and the thing as pure artifice. (p. 281)

Camp hesitates, then, between a signifier that is wholly arbitrary in its arbitrariness and a signifier the signified of which seems to be a meta-signifier—that the sign is a construct, that the sign means "sign." (Camp is "camp.") From the arbitrary on to artifice: but surely a signifier recognized as artifice, artefact, as construct is tautological. On the one hand, a sign in its potential to mean "anything," must float, indeed, even flutter, from signified to signified. On the other, camp is both made ("an artifice") and made-up. These two hands juggle so skillfully that the bright balls move so rapidly as to appear as one.

White cites particular works and authors in his notes but Djuna Barnes appears first of the single authors, a text all her own. Sontag considered Barnes one of her favorite authors and sent her a copy of *Against Interpretation* in which "Notes on 'Camp'" first appeared. Barnes wrote to Sontag in very Barnesian terms: "I have been informed that seeing me on the village streets, you have refrained from addressing me, because someone has told you that I am a Demon of some violence and invective. Please do me the pleasure of speaking to me the next time?" Barnes' biographer notes laconically: "Because of their mutual formality, they never met" (Herring p. 297, quoting Hank O'Neal p. 33).[v]

One might imagine *The Getty Fiend* as the monstrous spawn of an encounter that never took place between "a [purported] Demon of some violence and invective" and the woman who invented the idea of inventing camp. (Sontag notoriously asserts, "Yet one feels that if homosexuals hadn't more or less invented camp, someone else would" [Sontag, note 53, p. 291]).

Indeed, Sontag's one personification in note 16 is a meta-personification: "the Camp sensibility is one that is *alive* to a double sense in which some things can be taken" (emphasis added). To personify is to make the inanimate alive and Sontag personifies a "sensibility" as "alive": camp seems to require that the inanimate be alive twice over.

In a Golden Age of Zombies, *The Getty Fiend* reanimates that Camp sensibility. The fiendish vivacity with which White has called forth the vivacity of his fiend can stop the breath and the hearts of its readers. (As I have argued, it can break their hearts as well.) For White has done more than make camp come alive. Nor has White merely "reanimated" camp (as another zombie stumbling towards a niche market). His achievement is more remarkable.

Ken White's *The Getty Fiend* reinvents camp for the 21st century.

Michael du Plessis
February 2017
Los Angeles, CA

---

i. White notes, "The concept, intention, and occasion of *The Getty Fiend* is a distorted retelling of Marie Du France's le lai du Bisclavret, composted and compounded with Guy Endore's gothic horror pulp novel, *The Werewolf of Paris*, with the notable exception of featuring as its initial protagonist a storied Icelandic shapechanger from the Bronze Age—all set in contemporary Los Angeles" (p. 98). What he slyly neglects to signal is that Kvedulfur the "shapechanger" and Marie de France's *Bisclavret* all have lycanthropy in common with Endore's werewolf.

ii. "Nothing is spared because nothing is left unsaid" (p. 4), suggests Peter Brooks, for whom melodrama incarnates "the mode of excess" as his subtitle asserts. Melodrama involves "states of being beyond the immediate context of [a] narrative, and in excess of it" (p. 2). Peter Brooks, *The Melodramatic Imagination: Balzac, Henry James, Melodrama and the Mode of Excess* (New York: Columbia University Press, 1985).

iii. Sabine Baring-Gould's *The Book of Werewolves* first published in 1865, provides an essential guide. For Bisclavret, see p. 60, for Kveldulfur, see pp. 43-47 (London: Senate, 1993 rpt.).

iv. Susan Sontag "Notes on 'Camp'" in *Against Interpretation* (New York: Delta, 1966) pp. 275-292. The original publication date (1964) is noted at the end of the essay.

v. Hank O'Neal, *"Life is painful, nasty and short…in my case it has only been painful and nasty"* (New York: Paragon House, 1990) quoted in Philip Herring, *Djuna: The Life and Works of Djuna Barnes* (New York: Penguin, 1995). O'Neal appears to be the author of the remark about why the Sontag and Barnes were never able to meet (Herring p. 297).

.

the getty fiend

(a medieval melodrama in contemporary los angeles)

Dramatis Personae

KVELDULFUR: Prince of Cads, the Rightful Duke of San Vicente Avenue.

SORCHA: Duchess of Barrington, second in line for coronation.

KVELDULFUR'S ABSENCE: The Usurping Marquis; the Duke's ersatz advisor.

SORCHA'S QUESTION: Veritable interlocutor, pincer wielded under pince-nez.

THE RUNAROUND: The canyon complex of Sulci, a sly cartography of cortex.

THE ICONS OF SINAI: A broad and biased chorus.

ST. LUKE OF THE THROTTLED HALO: Your Momma so fat she eats Wheat Thicks.

THE ORIGIN OF THE TRUTH: An honest old counselor.

THE TRUTH: A savage and deformed slave.

THE NOTEBOOK: Peerless, blank.

THE READING LAMP: An Extra-Large Airy Spirit [courtesy of George Nelson.]

NYMPHS

REAVERS

WILL MUNNY: A cold blooded killer.

OTHER SPIRITS attending Kveldulfur.

THE GARMENT IN QUESTION: Pure occlusion, protean eclipse.

SETTING: The sea - *hey*, [the air - *ho*], with a laden merchant vessel; afterwards a coastal island of pale damascene consisting of a single absent plain   its void

well-defined by shapelessness

punctuated   by

blizzard, oblit-
eration.

prelude

[the getty center]

East elevation

                                          OVER BLACK:

RUSH OF WIND.

Faint symphony of CAR HORNS grows louder…

FADE IN:

EXT. HIGH ABOVE LOS ANGELES, <u>FALCON CAM</u> - CONTINUOUS

POV from tousled shoulders of a gliding peregrine.

BELOW:

The great sprawl. To the south juts ganglion cluster of shining
steeples. From a thousand feet up the gaze of the US BANK tower.

To the north, an unreadable postcard: HUGE WHITE LETTERS claim
hillbrow's de facto altar with inscrutable signifying idols.

Far ahead, scrim of haze, sepia and pink. Ocean's dim teal hem.

From distant west-most hilltop, a DISTRESS BEACON, toward which—

EXT. HOLLYWOOD TO BRENTWOOD - CONTINUOUS

—FALCON CAM accelerates.

SERIES:

—FRANKLIN becomes SUNSET, spice-trade route dark with pilgrims.

—BEVERLY CORRIDOR blurs to WESTWOOD VILLAGE, north to—

—monastic brick edifice of ABBOT ROYCE'S HALL, then—

EXT. THE GETTY CENTER - CONTINUOUS

—on a looming motte rests white-gold Camelot in fossiled block.
Banners snap in sea wind atop buttercream barbicans. Smooth
serpentine bailey gleams above broad green moat of succulents.

Lesser structures scatter the foliate hillside.

Locked in chain, segments of the endless millipede. Ten lanes
of besiegers strangulate the hill, grind unpredictable stop-and-
go patterns to baffle castle sentries, flash shields emblazoned
with battle cry in perpetuity: Interstate California 405.

ON THE PARAPET

Lady SORCHA, bedecked in Ann Taylor factory seconds, paces,
frets, smokes glass-wristed, her thick hair rank with clove.

Forge bellows stoke DISTRESS BEACON, Sorcha's discontent.

Below, a line of sappers, each cunningly disguised as an agent, a
costume designer, grip/crafty/transpo, disappears into its hole.

A sound like TEARING PAPER as—

—FALCON CAM DIVES, plummets right for, then

[wingtip kisses earlobe]

past [radiant brow] Sorcha [radiant root], sweeps over—

EXT. GETTY COURTYARD - CONTINUOUS

—fountains wetting rock formations. Lounging bronze statues.
Past garden view of terraced sunken amphitheater, rebar flowers
made of flowers, lime-green hedge-maze picked clean of coin.

Past marketplace HUBBUB, BARTERING over espresso rations.
Merchants BICKER over a pallet of blackmarket panini.

Through tall glass doors open for a snippet, a glimpse of the
GALLERIES, then shutter closes on an aisle of busts.

HUM of approaching drawbridge tram, laden with refugees.

EXT. GETTY RESEARCH PAVILION - CONTINUOUS

FALCON CAM wheels past scholars' cells, veers down a hidden
curvilinear path, hovers at alcove, RAPS.

With audible CRACK, wall surface sheds stone chips. A narrow,
handle-less door swings inward on silent hinges.

O.S. GURGLE, muted STRANGLE.

INT. COPYWRITER'S OFFICE, THE GETTY CENTER - MOMENTS LATER

Mad Men-swank meets Teddy Roosevelt-chic. Time capsule
hopelessly out of sync. Also parchment, scrolls, quill, wick
and tallow.

FALCON CAM brakes, comes to rest on a hand-carved bow perch
beside a tasseled leather hood, a terrarium of feeder mice.

Aperture blinks on empty walnut banker's chair.

O.S. SQUELP of compressed rubber. Incomprehensible GUTTURALS.

GRUNTS, STRAIN, A GROWL, FERAL PANTING…

part one

*[From Ceylon to Iceland and from Iceland to Ceylon,
all the old races have tales to tell of it.]*

—Guy Endore, The Werewolf of Paris

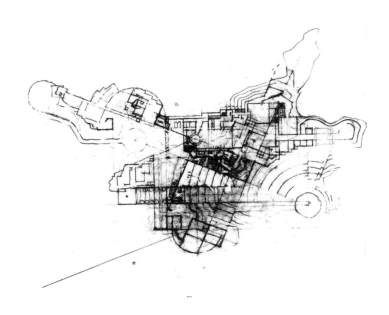

THE GETTY FIEND

Behold *The Beast* pinioned
on the racquetball, as terrible
in his agony as a mangled cuticle.

KVELDULFUR writhes to absolve
rhomboid wrench aggravated
by hard office chair. He needs

an Aeron but Aeron's too dear. He needs a jog,
some ice, four Advil, two beers—the formula
once could grow a lost limb back

or a salamander's tail. A taller desk might
suffice the interim. A taller vice might
tender diversion. Before concupiscent

Tudor upstarts the long-tined dynastic
salad forks of Plantagenet ran red. Now Verizon
works almost everywhere. Kveldulfur's trilby

punctuates coat tree, raffish with stingy
brim. Most pressing wish? Address
of braided ligament, although how limiting

the physical. As for the visual, how
derivative. Swivels pelvic girdle, sweet-talks
doorframe seam to spine, a single foot

opposes Knoll teak file cabinet—*The Beast* forthwith
aquiver with concentration. Glassy saline nougat
beads glossy citrine philtrum. Cuff's kissing row

functional faux horn buttons fans embers
of long dispute with foreign nation
of the present. What about a Spineworx?

A Teeter Hang Ups inversion table decked
with gravity boots? Or, scotch it, full swap—
a hidden key sentry gargoyle cast in resin?

It's a SkyMall classic. It's Hollywood Forever
all over Gower. Steady pressure, silversmooth
patter approaching prayer—the incredible force

required of counterpoise—when *click*, audible
shift, synovial release [as with all things, temporary].
Behold relief, *The Beast* suspended in mid-air.

The Duchess of Barrington Ave.

considers the Brazilian wax cleverest moiety
of rage. Smooth, now reddened, swollen

irreducible candor, her royal ardor, the slightest kiss
of air or brush of cotton-poly blend

abrades netherberry sunset
of clear-cut nether skin.

                          And from the dent
in the wall   the ersatz *office* of the J. Paul,

                                   tawny Sorcha

                               flexed

                                       mobius

strip, dappled apple of Dubai's
eye, principal of the stable, snorts, coy
mare, glances sidelong, tail held aside
backs Kveldulfur against the basement stair.

Her extraordinary bill. Her comely beak and queenly
proboscis. Singer Sargent's Madam X meets Madam
Ahkmatova in duel balanced on the bowsprit.

Sorcha's pistolero: bone china demitasse—hurled glove
onto his work surface as from the break room warbles
the interminable kettle. Loupe elides light table.

                                   [in arid high desert
                                   city: palms, alms
                                   and succulents, he longs
                                   for anything once met
                                   peat, smacks of fjord,
                                   not the least of which
                                   a snort of heady petrichor].

16

FLASH half-a-year, half-a-year, half-a-year FORWARD: into the tureen of breath rides…

THE SIX HUNDRED: DOOMED

Their shared condominium courtesy of such knockoffs
or real McCoys as could be found
up Topanga or couched in a Beachwood
cranny. Kveldulfur daily blesses the crone
who let go late husband's Barcelona chair—impeccably
tufted—for chump change. A candle burns for her
on the sill. Drizzled paraffin foots
her foil effigy. The Craigslist
eureka/bullseye had sent him

                                        into tizzy.
                                        How banal.
                                        How sublime.
                                        How fallen

into static—but for rapid shallow panting
in their Case Study platform bed—rosewood
veneer—sex so acrobatic that Kveldulfur

quite certain he'd tweaked his iliopsoas
semi-severely. Sorcha shone, a devotee
wrapping up with hot vinyasa, her spine

                                        torched conduit

still simmering. One open book from a stack of spine-spread
carcasses, partly devoured. Kveldulfur's perfect bedside notebook
in which he keeps

safe   his perfect
                    [PEERLESS]

                              and
end-
        less

                        snow-
                            field.

SOUNDS BEYOND LIMIT

of brief and bulky human tongue

> strike whole body's tin-
> tinnabulum.

Sorcha skewers his kidney-hatch with her manicure.

And to think last night when I woke
you were gone—

Kveldulfur turns a peerless page
to another soothing blankness

Goose-pimpled glass. What happened to the fabulous 70s thatch? I loved your
thicket—

I'll get you my pretty. *I know.* And your little dog, too.

Give it up. I was alone—

Vast and put-upon muliebral sigh. Cue flying monkeys.

So was I?

> [And thus the crossed swords of nonsense unfold.]

Precisely the Sleight of Tongue

that could turn a yard-long ash-shaft
before it violated muslin of plowman's shift

[the plowman having been pressed, as it were, into service,
as he had been, would have been grateful for it]. Almost flattering

in their ferocity
the Blood Ponies

of Tajikistan, the multi-
pede of Tamerlane un-

matched in hardiness.
Blah. Blech. She rolled

onto her hip. Across the savannah: her navel.
[below her belly two lions kissing

as they clasp]. Despite inguinal twinge,
he stirred. Sorcha flicked

his testicle.
He suppressed

the insurrection
of a flinch.

       Sorchaswoonsusurring—anvil presents broad hips
       for hammer—it's not *what* but *sound* of such. Witness

       headlong runaway livery cob full stride
       in arabesque. Does not your body blur

       just now so clearly that present skips
       the very moment when even familiar

       is made strange as it enters your ear?

Too much too deep too fast—let's retreat to the beginning.

THE MEET CUTE: THE ICONS OF SINAI

Modest champagne suit of modest Mediterranean cut
Kveldulfur's waistcoat justified only
by many pockets for many calibers of pen.

Waistcoat ink bandolero. From embossed shoulder holster
blank postcards amplify his pretense
to degree nearly unbearable

[To the Lord, no less. To the Lord.]

Sorcha a vision in gold foil, a song of praise
written on the frame, her hem. In the Old Testament
the three Magi appeared four times

[To the Lord, no less. To the Lord.]

Sorcha shows evidence of fine repair
to the damage in her lower parts,
possibly from much touching and kissing

[Of the Lord, no less…]

St. Luke had made her many times while on sabbatical
from the Lord, who dwelt then at the monastery, no less,
in Constantinople, renowned for the quality of its sandals

and for references in its public texts
to instances of forgery, and heavy petting
[By the Lord] more or less

while the bread and wine of the Eucharist
took sanctuary in the open mouths of supplicants,
from the ritual, no less, of the transformed.

ALL AT SEA

The forum, the piazza, the sun long past the yardarm,
over it he swung—an import hammock run amok—into
simultaneous crowd-wide croon stuffed mushrooms
cede delectable grease spots to table-linens—all dinner guests
are pointillists—and the smallest finger
of his leaf-shaped hand babbles dull
Morse on clouded tympana of plastic.
Deep burgundy box-wine

lens. Swan-prowed Sorcha
elides the grid
of wakes
a soignée blade   the very butcher

of Kveldulfur's acrylic button. If ever caravel
should bear far nearer spice-bearing wind
as tempera and silver leaf with glazes over gesso

into unsuspecting Sorcha's tiger-cowrie
ear, garlanded in coral:

       In Iceland, we call such prominent noses
       konganef. That's '*nose* of a *king*'
                 like that smirking Gaul
                   Vincent Cassel's.

Sorcha aspirates her truffle, hacks, fires feta crumble
through diastema, same fetching

broadside flintlock demi-cannon
as Brigadier General Lauren Hutton's—

       …further, at midsummer you can golf around the clock.

Sorcha lifts his foremost pocket flap,
into tweedy mail slot

deposits soggy missive. Olive oil
Rorschach. His colors fair
struck.

Transcendentally imbecilic, dearest top-flight imbecilette. Not only are you very bad at whatever was that lurching stunt, but in this arbitrary seaside hierarchy I'm also your immediate superior, now and henceforth, which makes you

ever so very worse.

The wind picks up
Sorcha makes sundry leagues
of profligate knots. Her crossover pure Hardaway—

tacking   tacking   tacking   tacking

Scotty beamed her up. Her quick first step outshone
vintage Allen Iverson [He's talking about

practice. Practice? Talking about practice!
Notagame Notagame Notagame

Practice?]

Kveldulfur clutches at the iron straw
he'd driven through his tongue.
Sorcha shrugs, a candle-flame
past an open doorway.

[She'd witched him, a glass shiv,
left him sputtering
into empty space as lungs
struggled to fend
marine layer creeping in.
Kveldulfur afire in pink froth
pulls paper scrap, precious
trifling pen—a thumbless
assassin fumbling
his trifling shuriken]

Exeunt.

THE DAY JOB:

Habit, a soul too weak to have tight grip
on its body, only a wilder form of caress
than he'd hitherto practiced, a tiny guillotine.

With all the care of a government trapper
allotting his beeswaxed set, Kveldulfur situates
billet-doux outside Sorcha's cubicle, glances up
to instep, gathered tuck of incarnadine

       Hera pumps, sale rack

          at Saks.

To whit:

In this harvest of data, I weld the tone
of light as bar wipes clean the much abused
glass of Xerox machine, the lacework bridge
you build for me of invisible lacework bricks—

Mercy! Beg mercy. Mercy—Sorcha intervenes, finger raised, a Swiss voulge
at hover above the begrimed nape of Charles the Bold,
tubercular Duke of Burgundy, who succumbed
as it were, to a well-placed [as it had been] and timely
stroke, absence of actual tuberculosity notwithstanding.

If cannonfire over broad blank field
of my own distance there remains rumpled
night my fair absence of acceptable I.

Sorcha's facemap: *floored* and blinked mildly
to prove it, hooded eyes broody
as a Fonda's. Shhhh, baby. *Shhhhh…*

Don't make me chase you—even doves have pride…?
Falters as he fades. Way to wield the poleaxe, nimrod.

Chronic suppuration of virulent idiocy. She pats
his shoulder with her misericord.
In say, commiseration, like.

POST-GAME: THE OBSERVATORY

He was ashamed. His heart's harangue
infected with misplaced rhetoric, himself awash
in effluvia of pear-husks.

[parks his old Saab 900 where?]

Actually, he was himself half-ready to believe
no doubt about it. He had been bewitched, else
how could he have been wangled into such

[engages the slope how? The broad trail: turbocharged. Turbo.]

compromise? This one has neither beginning
nor end—not true; he heard halloos of drunkards
bedevil sweating avenues. Something overturned

[a dumpster? A Mini Cooper? In-N-Out paper cup of ice?]

in every alley. Sin is always the same, a discussion
between parroting mimes over onion soup
and leftover au jus. Wanton. His third tallboy
of Hite smuggled from The Prince.

[Foliate streets: the live oaks and wild oaks. The mustached mistresses
                                                of Griffith Park]

Kveldulfur swallowed into pixelated trees, such as
they were, not quite as they had been, nor ever
storied endless orange groves over valley's hillbrow
orange groves reputed once ranging free all the way
to redwood groves of fern-rich north. From trains
with fowling pieces Eastern travelers once
slew citrus in droves for sport.

MAGISTER LUMIERE

Rightly so there came verily by the holy telescope
at roost over the spangled worm of Western
Avenue in its sinuous gold-lit gossamers and lurid stoplights
and brake lights and green lights and come-hither headlights
the evening gown of the ball python, marigold and lavender.

A mile or more. There, beside the bench
at hairpin's reverse, an oaken-haired man
knelt in the likeness of a holy vessel   an Easy Bake Oven
and before him in pinafore   eyes pressed shut in rapture

stood one of the likeness of an angel–
Strawberry Shortcake, my you're looking swell—who bolted,

hitching up his drawers. Anon, as Man-God and as supplicant
the kneeling called out: Come forth and thou shalt see

that thou hast much desired to see.
Then began to tremble   Then held up his hands

licked pursed lips: Hist! Lime Chiffon! Now wottest thou what I am?
[Notebook challenged for the throne of blank]

I thought not—yr an uncommonly thick meringue—saith the goodly man

[Then he donned
a mackintosh of red sendal,
mayhap by YSL, mayhap
by D&G, and bare a
mantle upon his shoulder
that was furred with
marten or with mink—lined
in the high and ridiculous
Burberry plaid—he'd seen
all grown and smoking *hot*
smoking fucking hot
Hermione Granger in the
ad—and the leer knight
said unto the blear knight:
Sirlet, my stunned
confection, do attend...]

St. Luke of the Throttled Halo

Overlooking the northbound 5 a sliver of the Zoo
off the trail a chapel much worse the wear for its abuse,

its own hem also much kissed and fondled. This is, saith the flaxen man,
hair a nimbus, hair a Burchfield moonlit dandelion, the richest thing

any rogue or gent hath living. [And anon there in clove-dark rotted ghost
of window sash and carbon frame the miter a bit of frost

out of season in the antechamber—The Garment in Question
nudging from branny soil]. No club door will be closed to you. Henceforth

all your tickets will be comped.   Do you wish to part the curtains
of The Falcon?   All thread bows its head to cloth.

I once buried this with mine own hands in the city of Antioch [near unto Syria]
with uncommon zest   for evangelizing fangs

[when said mantle crosses your shoulders your sleep
shall be murdered with revel] saith the good man of Antioch
        Once of Syria.

        [Lo, a spirit seizeth him
        by spine-root and he suddenly
        crieth out, and throweth
        him down, his arms aflail]
        Pinging blows and flicks
        at his clavicles [he weeps?] so that
        he foameth from his crown
        indigo gore [verily,
        a fount] and 1-2-3, 1-2-3, bruising
        his zygomats, dinging his heel-
        caps upon the hardness of the air
        he hardily departeth from the
        hardness of the ground 2-3-4,
        2-3-4

And   *Cha-cha-cha*   flit   inseam snit

        Cha-cha-cha

Chapel-dee, chapel-da   Kveldulfur left baching it.

THE GARMENT IN QUESTION

As for the marten, the sendal hint, it obscured itself, a breeze zipped
in untouched brass. In a gale in a trice it buttoned over that, a single row
of treated snaps or two rows arrowed to either side of breast. And epaulets
as occasion demands—or belted, placketed, buckled, reinforced
and triple-stitched. It caught woes in a pocket
for sections wrapped in ribbon, A-F.

Bivouac bag, the cradle, or the cross. Gray gabardine?
Sometimes waterproofing wax, though the gloss had gone.
If derizon slung sleet through leafless trees
the whole of it a hooded cape with telescoping
poles. When hail, ice eggs shrinking to grains
of rice, and car interior bakes forgotten Pomeranian,
then a thing all mesh and grommets.

Whether Solomon confined in the warp with sigils
and other such arcane formulae the odd half-dozen

incubi remains uncertain. Whether his favorite old testament
background actor fresh from central casting—god the natty

tailor—whipped a little something frothy up, a little
something-something streamlined and bespoke—a satin geyser

from abalone [for luster] and hawser frayed
from hawsehole [for grit], then concealed it

before he fell upon Nebuchadnezzar
and was sore aggrieved, is a bit up in the air as of yet.

However it Came to be it Came to Bind Him

Lastly, Kveldulfur shed Puma hightops of patent-leather
also he did constellate on his helm, of which he had naught,

which he then decamped for the shrub. All in pantomime, like.
Shield would he take none, as he was full nude. If in fact

shield his charge and field would be that of The Knight
of the Blizzard, purest quintessence of pallor

[overlay: squall of freckles. A microburst]

Then he took up a marvellous spear.

Then he lay it by.   Slew a field-vole

with his plowshare.

                      [Right so he did; the queen was in her tower
                      with all her ladies lit

                      by what seemed the bookend
                      afire a crown of tapers. Right so

                                      there sprang forth
                      as if girded to do combat, girded in paraffin,

                      girded in beetle shells of candied viridian,
                      the holy vessel—a fair guess—of the garment

                      with all manner of sweetness and blades
                      and still more manners of savor].

part two

[In those days, he was hard pressed to satisfy that hidden appetite
which he had only recently come to understand clearly.]

—Guy Endore, The Werewolf of Paris.

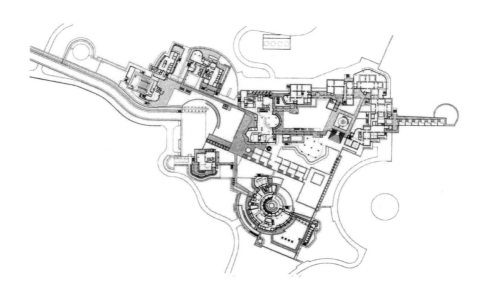

LULLABY FOR A MARIONETTE

Forsooth. That is: a caterwaul. How to begin
if in fact to begin at all. The impulse is to focus

on the string and how it wears
thin or how it shapes the fingers or the fingering.

Or the joinery in fact involved in such a simple thing
as shoulder, folded crocus, or in the shouldery, the shouldering

glint of nails, manipulator [*manipulator!*] hidden or revealed,
by digits built of flint. By hambone. By foxed lint.

As I say: forsooth. That is, not all is lost or misplaced. The prince
of my dreams has been made into boots. The kingdom: erased.

EXT. HOLLYWOOD BOWL AMPHITHEATRE, LOS ANGELES - NIGHT

En plein air.

A GIGANTIC TV SCREEN perches over an orchestra imprisoned in
carved shell wings. Hillside crowded with the picnicking rapt.

Tuxedoed galley frees Wagner's Valkyries into June dark.

The cheap seats. In the rear wall's shadowed seam a dense-furred
BEAST hugs earth, motionless but for hackle-rise, lung-fall.

ONSCREEN, a bright bronze keg in horned helmet. ELMER FUDD, 50s,
warbles his dewy, soft-R'd battle cry, plunges his spear into
a rabbit's hole with a plumber's enthusiasm for a clogged drain.

C.U. SCREEN: Fudd in league with glee, in thrall to wrath.

                    FUDD (sings)
                Kiww the waaabbit (x3)

BUGS, white-gloved slim coquette in pale gray, postures, glib.

                    BUGS
                Kill the rabbit?

                                              CUT TO:
EXT. JAGGED MOUNTAIN PEAK - LATER

At distance, Fudd's antic form silhouetted against an iron sky.

                    FUDD
            And I'll give you a saaaammmmple!

Armored Fudd's wild paroxysm a kinesthetic spell. His maestro's
seizure invokes thunder, torrent, wind.

WIDE ANGLE:

                    [Gustavo Dudamel plies airy forces
                    with a supple reed. Sable curls
                    riot unrestrained. Bows rise and fall
                    in unison, shower crowd with hurtling
                    notes-on-fire invoking spasm. Mass carnage
                    in the ranks. The Beast packs it in.]

LIGHTNING immolates the elm near Bugs. Charred lapine ears wilt.

                                              CUT TO:

IN A SHALLOW TROUGH

The accordion unfolds—attend: before this, in bowered
byways, long before, say, when rather than odd affliction
the odd half-dozen lice apiece were simply a condition
of existence to be borne among husks and rushes
of ersatz boudoir, poached furs a worn forest
too defoliated to hold off wind. In this former time
[a quieter time] among siblings crammed for warmth
against cob walls, heaped on pallets on the packed dirt
floor, long winters were filled with many possibilities
for variegated end by night or short cruel day.

No penicillin, for one. Intravenous Lactated Ringer's Solution
also sorely lacking.   Angioplasty techniques a bit rustic yet.

                              These very real concerns

[Infection, spirits, vapors, injury, an imbalance
of choleric humor, an abscessed tooth.]

As real as our very real concerns
[kidney donor list, melanoma, 501(c)3 status, a kickass central gaming
console, the best cell phone plan that includes wireless internet and digital
cable]. What is this? Yes, BUNDLING, etc. how many donor list followers,
etc. are following #terminalrenalfailure, et al? Who understands the origin of
the pound sign used in this or any such identifying capacity?

                              [Manye a poure scoler telles howe
                              thro tymes travelles
                              divers mysteryes]

HAIL MARY

Each soldier-cricket entrenched in timothy casts back
to stars its rhythm-divinity. Every grass stalk of the field

commands one silvered vertical district, heralds
a herd of Eland? Oryx? Kudu or Hartebeest?

Eland. Arrival of a hundred or a hundred fifty
confirmed Eland, proud as ink, save for eggshell

hand-span at throatlatch and a chain of red-wrought
gold to the full broad width of the forehead

of the high-pated haruspex murmuring
over entrails clasped around each spiraled ebon

horn by horsehair-clasp in heavy plait, by the jeweled bell-
tone tree-note of a treeing redbone or trailing black-and-tan.

Titles with a Dagger are Reviewed Above

Beside the Garment in Question, Kveldulfur, Knight
of the Tousle, wakes in loud and tousled pile
of last year's plantain.

How, like a novice shaken from long vigil
over some other squire's arms and altar

> throws off
> the stiffened posture
> of early hours
> throws off
> new hauberk and
> embroidered tunic

> [throws off favors
>   promised
>
> to his distant lady

> for the favor of the near and torpid breeze
> embroidering his naked skin].

RETURN TO THE KEYBOARD

Few or nil have witnessed such astounding feats
of words-per-minute—letters
themselves all ink-in-a-grand-mal astounded fit
to arrive in, inhabit a body, sans serif. Every detail
crystalline slow-motion—suspicion: Kveldulfur sniffs
his mug for Adderall, in any case undetectable. Sorcha huffs
and puffs and blows down his door, always
as she well knows, open. Harps with considerable aplomb
on arbitrary tardiness, in full-scale inspired upbraid.

Kveldulfur presses coracle ear to iMac screen's new retina display.

> Hear that? My copy sings. You are so pure
> a marvel that you are unaware of being a marvel—

Sorcha warps in sovereign grip: https:// time slips:

> *Speak not more lies,*
> *Grim hamrammr! Grim*
> *Skallagrim! The ring-*
> *giver grows*
> *weary of*
> *her foe, unworthy*
> *defiler of*
> *swan-road's*
> *blade!*

Then bit down   Whoa. Whoa. *What?*   Sorcha bit down

hard on Kveldulfur's left deltoid and his perineum
clutched, bloomed Aurora Australis of the spasming
satchel, he—not to put, in good faith, too fine
a very fine point on it—*came*, the humming ache, broken bow
string's first wrist-slap. He'd thought himself beyond
surprise but christalmighty the flood.

As suddenly she spat him out—freckled brawn, his spit-damp
broadcloth, her pupils wide black
catcher's mitts, her mouth still gaped—spat him out
a mouthful of so many
melting Skittles, fled.

So absolute
a miracle

So absolved

the mark of solicitude throbs exertion, contention, the throes
of PEERLESS agonism, *seize* it, a knife-pinch. He springs

> unaware of every lung-bellow/lung-bellow
> miracle below.

> [that night the toothmark
> bruise a child's drawing
> of a lashless open
> eye, in stenciled aubergine,
> with little gap at top.]

Matrimonial Toast:

My dear near-to-hearts, commoners and peers, miscreants,
Cluniacs and other such habitués, the day of my wedding
is every day. Let us be thankful for the long
perpetually animate hands of John Berryman

tweaking the guylines of his Pal, Mr. Bones. And let us hope
that if he were here he might extend that glorious pallor
of his index finger, that skeletal and elegant baton
toward the podium to bless this union
                                        over here
                                                and other such wonders
                                                    we're sitting on.

[The uncertain polite mutter
crowd-wide elaborates
into halting percussive flapping soon
suppressed.]

IN ABSENTIA:

All mistakes heal in time and those that do not
do not. Kveldulfur quite resigned

to grazing bluegrass to bluegrass
seed—he lolled. He loafed and leaned

in remembrance of that bearded libertine
and showed likewise knack, sitting silently electric

for hours, accumulating his invisible fortune, another sham.
Sorcha passed her open hand across the back of the divan.

Sometimes he was much shaken by her absence
of ardor the blank left where once dwelt

their injurious striving. Terrific cardio. Pied-
montese. Pure USDA Grade A #1 prime

beef all the way to heel—dream cattle kneel
dreaming in very real stalls.

Dress Code for Shaving

Mid-hunt, the stag of self
inches from his grip while rank and file

of pack [the self divided] harry fast
at flank—the faintest waft of mint-

and-eucalyptus always good for that. At bay
at last doomed sultan swings

tangled rack, drives adder-headed spades
into diamondbacked gap. Behold *The Beast*

jaws wide in flight! Triumphant
collision—lopsided nose smear

maligns bathroom mirror. Ensuing silver
bite, then scarlet plumbline from gouge

to clavicle. Flexes red-centered
medallion, scrapped hemostatic

toilet paper hinge. Catalyzed mid-stride
panting troupe collapses, putrefies, then erupts,

unflags banners in red-orange, mantled black
and fully multiple, marches silent drums a clutch

full onslaught of Monarch butterflies hatch
of midges hatch of warblers mist of flying

beetles. In full bloom wet-flanked stag trembles
in the leg, nostrils disced, antlers bedecked

in tangerine and sable, heaves in small-lunged
wind, flutters [vermilion] alder leaves [black].

THE FIX

Sails in over SF valley to LAX from coppiced Oaktown
little L-shapes forged from stucco, scattered catbox

litter, stippled stenciled kidney beans, brilliant
rectangles, vivid copper-foxing tourmaline. Bright day

Kveldulfur became just like that—stucco patch on textured
stucco wall. Red-clay tile on red-tile roof. Face it, lavender

is lavender. Scent hates so hard on its liegelord flower,
revolts to join nighttime alley bloom's

greasy paper, tarred asphalt, stairwell piss-and-liquor
adjacent—each age of scent

births riddles, eats some, hides others
for later. Delicious groin pong

of musk and oil, civet lure at freshly lathered
epicenter. Famished scent commas nudge

at stunted muzzle. Months pass. An old blind tailor
mends the nets. Despite the plan

no two dropped bread crumbs
manage to align, though gold-gutted hen

bleeds secrets through her stitches—blink,
the mouthless harp spills six-toed ginger Manx

from vinyl bean bag's persimmon lap.
Kveldulfur bears the common weight

of daytime's loveliest wrath
made sore wroth, pearl-skin

over cuttle-fish ink, memory skin
over pearl-body, coral reflection

against underpink hue and now silver, now sun-gold
peering through as blank voyeur or as peerless

master just another fragment
of the invisible

keeping syncopation at bay, never
overtly syncopating.

COEUR DU BOIS

After more gonesome days measuring a quarter-score,
give-or-take, the trick was in convincing Sorcha

that the columns that record the score
the wins and losses total the net sum

of tire-sipes, snow-studs, or clay-scores
that make the cleaving-to and joining

something exceeding a cut-rate background score
to a plotless story: pastel, murder-free

Noir, fedora-less, in which nobody scores
with no dames. Nobody squashes no grapefruit

in nobody's face. It's simply not in the dance score—
dahhling, a bit of soft-shoe, some razzle-dazzle misdirection

to prove that there had been no diminishing, score-
less, feebling of devotion, but *damn*, he's not *always*

out of cell service—or at least by her count, the raw score
consistently two days each week untransformed, sometimes

three, [her application for keeping score]
purely gone as if abducted—a Bermuda Trinity.

SORCHA'S INKLING

What can she be? Who is willing to get him off
in the crook of her elbow? His quirks. The genius emerges; she

is her match. A workshop [the worship, the warship] her lie,
and so umbilical a license, that studio sky. Though she binds

her feet with sandals   cords bite into her ankles
so slim and redolent still   of depilatory gel.

Sorcha watches the LA Philharmonic, DVR-ed,
on a new 52" flat screen with sound turned down

                        has coin-bank Parson's Russell figurine
                                        as sentry

                        on her heirloom Victor-Victrola.

It comforts her somehow to eat unsalted Saltines
as Gustavo Dudamel [again! The Billboards!] plies the airy forces
with his supple reed. Glossy sable curls [they never end!] riot

            unrestrained. Foam-flecked horses
            blush froth over bone snaffles

            as mantis-wristed Dudamel flicks rearmost wings
            from his tethered brace of dragonflies

            with a bullhide quirt. He's propped aloft
            by manic stitching

            of rosined bows. Chariot wheels rimmed
            in rusted steel. Imperial girl by the handful

            casts from her basket of caramels answers
            to the severalled open mouths

            of Portuguese sailors who could not swim—
            that is, all of them—arms of the lost Armada,

            muted bells of the brass section. Sorcha warbles slightly
            through her nose. She had quit the violin.

THE WAY TO ARCADY: A CURE

Sorcha clicks across the parking structure to the waterfall
escalators at The Grove. Directions from wisest bearded biddies

cloistered in labyrinth of Farmer's Market: face
Johnny Rocket's. Crab-walk toward the tower clock

to receive—scrolled on paired hair-pins—sought affidavit,
pressed against chartreuse bruise on stockinged shin.

Review after a whisk through Anthropologie, the sales
nook, bins of glass drawer pulls and iron coat hooks

surveilled by plaster fashionista, airbrushed saucy mannequin. Sorcha
glosses prescription in rear corner of the Apple Store.

A Species of Melancholie

You may recognize such persons
by these marks; they are pale and thirsty. They have freckles

like pats of butter or bran flakes or bacon spatter. The point
is freckles—be *en garde* against the speckled man.

[no, she does not have questions about the new MacBook Air]

Give the patient a diet of mixed greens from the Whole Foods
salad bar then open a vein, abstract such blood unto fainting.

If Whole Foods too distant substitute from Trader Joe's an entire quart
of the green tea ice cream, now discontinued. For three days

let afflicted submerge in baths of Smart Water and whey protein, then
with stringy gourd-heart, slivers of Hakeem's Dream-shake, purge

such swarm of clung defenders with up-and-under and cold compress
of sheep's urine and sweet vinegar. As beverage, porcupine quills

and guard hairs, the ground forehead whorl from swirled bolt-stop
of polled cattle fattened on trillium. Disguise refreshment

of chronic cases by vomiting with hellebore. In the case of disease
full-formed, simply swab tonsils with opium

[Browsing. Just browsing just browsing. Browsing: just browsing, thanks.]

then polish them. To the patient, while in chains [and womens'
beards, and birds' spittle] grant such wholesome food as he requires.

After further purging, to be neither overlooked nor gainsaid, use again
adder's paste of honey, venom, and besotted ill-acted parlor charades. Add

poultice of prickly-pear [like when the hogs got lil' Arliss] and administer
those things aforementioned. Also administer liberally a few select

from among those things not mentioned, only this time
as random injectables. If necessary, the cautery.

THIS ART HOLDS THE ARTIFICER IN SUSPENSE

Sorcha in flattering half-light flaunts
hawklike profile against twinned rows
of illuminaria lining Santa Monica
Promenade with marked-down scented Xmas candles.

St. Luke performs as tramp with a crewelwork patch
knit to each knee, as hobo with three tick bird
barrettes perched in his mane, dressed all
gold-on-red, bone rattle tambourine.

> ST. LUKE (O.S.)
> It's said that in Senegal they sneeze
> in susurrant Senegalese. *Wolof.*

Luke jingles nickels in his upturned hat. Sorcha turns lyric of her V-lined back.

> ST. LUKE (*Sotto Voce*)
> It must be devastating
> to have been so publically handsome
> for so long. Then the first gray pube.

Sorcha, cornered shieldmaiden, brandishes iPhone as warding talisman.

> SORCHA
> My ride! I'm just waiting for my ride!

St. Luke drops the gag, advances now outfitted according to ecclesiastical rank, hips aswivel, a flamberge blade. Above vanity Tart Arnels rocks vintage tiara of the ever-evolving papacy.

> ST. LUKE
> I only meant Rupert Everett, the panic
> induced by a failing jawline, one imagines.
> It happens to all of us, almost. Positively terrifying...

Sorcha's gaze deeply taxed by seconds. *Oh. My.* Such
a skinny tie. Luke bows deeply from his tapered waist

then shifts pixels, pulls slow fade
into contra-limelight. Fragmented

about the savannah, the deathbed
scoured almost entirely clean,

St. Luke pictures a family of itinerant jackals
cavorting within an elephant skull, wants

to cough back the indigestible
parts, like a twilit owl, but not before

invoking bass 4/4 rumble of the late Emperor
of Exmoor, his shaggy spectral court

of candelabraed highland stags
cantering slantwise headlong

over Sorcha's chest, evidence
of passage the parceled mess

of sharp-edged hearts
carved in turf.

CONCERN IN D MINOR

What does he consume, when he is far from me? On zinc-topped
central bar Sorcha's special paring Henkel
categorizes heirloom tomato. Ripe avocado slices
part, buttery last-call thighs. Kveldulfur's boss dab hand
extended only yea far into the holy realm of culinary
excellence or concern—about as far
into that kingdom as blending a protein shake
in her industrial Cuisinart blender, the modern
funeral urn. Though nuances of her famous guac
eluded him, if he added fruit and protein powder it begat
a muddy species of smoothie, and thus Kveldulfur
was, thrust hard against the limits of his self-
sufficiency—or so she opined—starved or near
to starving, unless he had electricity.

[Flaunts the safety orange
pull cord of her   cunningly
long cuffed selvedge
her denim so   raw

so raw   in periphery
narrow frame of the panoramic
window slot—pale blur drops
past—no doubt a hawk's
hooks convulse knuckle-deep
in wet pelt

To the window! To the wall! To the
window! To the—only wind-felled
palm leaf to curbside, street
sweeping every second Monday.]

PERMISSION TO CROSSPOST

"Rocko." Six-year-old
Fawn pug. Needs meds.

Missing: Sasha—Chihuahua/pom
mix. Last seen 10/13 near Hamilton
and Alabama. Reward.

LOST: Cleo the Schipperke
slipped her collar
on her poor dog-sitter
yesterday and is lost
in the area of Woodbine
north of 16th Avenue
in Markham. She's about
12 lbs, shiny black coat,
pointy ears and nose, and
no tail. Call me anytime,
day or night if you see her
at 647-555-9481.

Permission to crosspost.

COMPASS ROSE

Sorcha couldn't cop to wanting
wired amp variable toggle
in her wa-wa pedal, the hot ceramic shard
of every halberdier embossed
on every conceivable surface
beneath the hound's-tooth surface
of her pencil skirt, and yet…

His winged helm, his cornsilk braids. Luke illustrates how a man can
simultaneously intimidate and sashay. For instance, in *Troy*, recall the perfect
pillars of Brad Pitt's legs—

> ST. LUKE
> Until you've harvested from the heaving chests
> of an entire Macedonian vanguard
> their chambered fading firebrands
> cut quivering whole from whole cloth
> you haven't really lived, I've always said.

Him… *Him.*   Sorcha offers ribs for the rib-spreader, sponsors her own
combustible.

> SORCHA
> I suppose you must lose a dog or two
> to earn a boar's head…

Sorcha wets parched lips. Luke pulls a pulled rabbit
Papperdelle from his hat of peppered

rabbit-felt, summons an airy municipality
of ethereal calligraphers

to trace spiralled symbols over folded
vellum, cartography

mottled with garnet droplets
dredged from the tepid Euphrates.

> ST. LUKE
> Quite. Circumstance calls for the subtle art
> of textile subtraction, the ramifications
> of which occasionally dire. No doubt

you have questions, no doubt. No matter.
When you arrive, I'll text you instructions.

Luke slides crimped parchment into inside pocket of Sorcha's Bottega Veneta
blazer, lets fleshy pads of his long hand linger, taps her inner button with his
index finger.

ST. LUKE
Meanwhile, as supplicants
to a supple throne, let us
improvise our lubricants…

GARMENT IN THE PROCESS OF BECOMING

Sorcha enters stage front, motheaten alibi, man-musk gentle
croquet mallet battering red-with-white-stripes croquet ball

into Kveldulfur's bright expectant bright front bright
front teeth. Numb at first. There's that at least. Of the weavers

capable of repairing french linen there are seven
surgeons of the threaded scalpel and of the living

who can count them? Curled in their swan-chair, a relative
bargain, Sorcha piles her hair onto her crown incidentally

still on fire much as the atomics of Abyssinia and the Egyptian Sudan
are credited with the power at will of becoming

hyenas—it's kind of not a very flattering angle
this moment in our relationship. Dropsy, the butchered

bull, conscripts his every molecule:

KVELDULFUR

I am, how to put it without
concomitant melodrama, a beast—kind of

the ultimate in cross-dressing only
you wouldn't believe how passing
it makes me. Total chromosomal
charade only I can never fully recall

which drag I'm performing. Choose any dove
in the cage collapsed, it's all an illuminated act

of translation complete with medieval
lettering, as common, really, as eating–

SORCHA

To say that I have met
rather, someone has reached

out to/into me—I am myself,
have never felt—how it is
possible that my skin
departs frame and each cell

unspools until every spiral
lies straight. Then as if

the sea? Some vast roar...

[Listen/*listen*, my love/*my love*, it's not the sound/*the sound*]

but the form of such—does not my body blur   peel   flay
reveal familiar final shape—

He's not\has never :: will never/listen.   Sorcha vibrates as gearshift deranges
manual transmission, excises   nobody's fool

from particular space. Of living reavers her mathematics
most spectacular. Laceration all that remains.

SORCHA'S DECISION

What does it mean to say a righteous queen
flew in tight formation, leaning on her wings?
Let's just say that Sorcha struggled against the gears
of daylight in reverse to steal some room
to plant carrageenan seeds on a sea
of loam, the field of St. Luke's
opened palm. Light fled, but night
was better mounted. Taking root, her eyes, limned
with lampblack, the power to reduce, affixed to sea-side
centuries of lichen, rendered themselves
all the better to see you with, my dear.

        Day smacks
               very sultry indeed, a heavy fox muffler
               nine yards long, weight of bombazine
               weeks ahead of any season. Sorcha's atrocious
               inbox chime. As carved tablet delivered
               in guise of touchscreen the Lord spoke. No choice
               more damning or replete ever lain curled
               at decision's feet, to be abandoned
               or plucked from the leaf-stacked lee
               of wasted rubble and cement foundation.

               But as for the whole of it [cretonne,
               Drap-de-Berry, etamine]
               in its multitudinous entirety,
               [organza, mousseline, sarsenet]
               its expansive charade,

                    [an arm swathed
                    in white samite
                    that caught him by his
                    hilt, and brandished him
                    three times, and drew him
                    under in the mere]

               it fit easily

               into her Kate Spade tote.

part three

[He left the body and ran back. There was no time to be lost...
He almost wished that his clothes wouldn't be there.]

—Guy Endore, The Werewolf of Paris

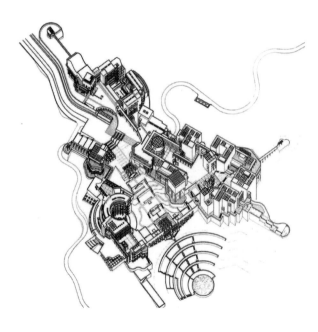

THE LIFE OF THE BEAST

Halos throttled of pepper, burred like teasel. Halos
the breath devises in tinny bangles. LASIK-eyed,

the odds-on dark contender trots shifting aisles,
listing bells of memory, centuries, tipples plastic towers.

Distant unseen spools recall   [
all-realm time chord. Strobe.   [
Booked headshot session.   [
Strobe. Strobe clone. Soft box   [

mylar bounce, 2-3 wardrobe   [
changes. For wardrobe   [
changes you pay   [
[charges] extra or nothing   [
changes but when
you depart the studio your
change purse once fat with
change lies slack

]   Margin shoulder lurking
]   mint Crown Vic
]   cherry whoop-whoop
]   poised eddied pike

               lurks the overpass
               shadow   cherrycherry
               Melrose squeal brings down
               whole hog house. Behold

]   the trembling glove/glaive
]   suspended   presenting
]
]   assault by   four-muscled
               stain flight   takes fleet
               hope in-   cessant feathers
               cramp as   rumor
               to his throat   until
               lips part with   urge with
               urge with   cavalcade
               of down   spill
               winged   belch

THE NEW ORTHODOXY

Harlow Gold and Cloister Black
the full extent of his Crayola set.

Also purple bearded darnel, a species
of rye-grass, the seeds of which

a soporific poison, grows plentifully
in Palestine. Add that verdant blue

David Hockney up and claimed
then called it quits, though enameled

lilies retain their freshness
for some time.

St. Luke of the Throttled Halo

Member him? Is mighty hung, friends. And golden.
The Virgin of the Burning Bush, he set afire
her altar. Her petals and the bush flamed after.

The apostle Peter tried—don't make me laugh—the apostle
Peter made efforts great and grave both to discourage St. Luke
from profligate ways also to beat him at cards. Luke trounced him

in Damascus. Borrowed his consort in Tarsus. Cured him
of syphilis in a hovel in Cyprus. He knotted his contrary Cypriot
snare, snugged it. Peter laved his feet in tears and kisses.

NEBUCHADNEZZAR'S ROOKIE YEAR

Stand anywhere you look there used to be a tree
threw down pine needles oak leaves
avocados margaritas what you wanted slid down

the bar into your hand—*slap!* You could kick it
sprawled among lionesses lazing with the lemurs
and gaze up at undercarriages of kingfishers. You could nap

among tumbled meercats. Yeah, Neb had to cut that shit down, stat.
He was a king. He had a saw. He did not generate
Original Ideas. Luke swaggered in his enameled codpiece

and with sonic boom and bright battering
spade razed promise to a bare stump. The party
was over. Puckered sap. The stump bound

with bronze, alone in its grassy field, St. Luke thought
it might make a pretty swell picnic table once it took on
a little patina. Oxidize! Oxidize thou thy bindings! Luke

snickered. He got a load of himself. He really ought
to take that show on the road, but first! A horn section!
Some percussion! Luke largely liked to dress as a cross

between Brandon Flowers with his peacock shoulders
and Planters salted peanut's Mr. Peanut—top hat, spats,
monocle, watch swinging from its watch chain,

and Luke always backed by big brass:

'Cause I've got   *BAM!*   [personality].
<u>Walk</u> [like Deuteronomy].
<u>Talk</u> [with calamity].
<u>Smile</u> [it's all vanity].
<u>Charm</u> [works like Dramamine].
Love [tuba drowns mouthed words].
An' plus I got a great big *har-ar-art!*

Down polished burlwood
                              the original Killer

                                                            slides his singular shiv.

The Cost of Doing Business

St. Luke frisked the Lord's bedside drawers and frolicked
in his bath—while the Lord's away, St. Luke—
well, St. Luke pretty much did what he wanted
in any event, tenancy of the Lord or no. If he so chose
to blitz horseback full speed through hallways
of box-stores or woodland thickets for
seven nights and seven days mucking underbrush
tearing off fresh cedar branches whipping nests
of tanagers from their nooks just for chuckles
at shell spray, and various devices from wireless docks
for shits and high-pitched giggles, then Luke did as much
and after a groom took his lathered horse he groped
the groom who wasn't even handsome, only intact
and in the way, and as he loved to do, quoted himself,
his truest gospel: *when I am a girl, a woman is considered
as strong as a man*, then slept another sweet sleep
a full night on the clean sheets of the entitled.

ANNEXED

Which made the time of changes a time of boiling
in his jaws and in his loins—a time which knew
no end, the Vesuvius in his head, plume
breaking train-smoke sky stirred him
to shred plastic bottles for polar fleece.
How popped plum cap twists
barrel of his lipstick slot, mulberry
moon unit. Sorcha's getting panelled
torques him, evidently, in hegemony
of binary regime. It's not yours, but get
over it; it's only cock, and fair play, it must be said
St. Luke's a top boy, witnessing the evidence,
at delivering the length. And by what miracle
had Sorcha become the famished queen
of spectacular head? She's a force. She's a genuine wonder
twice crowned of Aquitaine. Kveldulfur had lapped her
for hours dialling rotary phone upstream
against one and two o'clock, rolling
one lonely BB in figure-8s across the wall
just to bring her off, played the long con
then little snelled hooks set. Pommel horse?
Now St. Luke's reversed into single leg swing
routine—moores and spindles flow into Thomas
flairs. His ground work, crownwork and…
Lumineers? All-round caps? He laughs, travels expertly
counterclockwise Sorcha's ecstatic
apparatus. Wedding cake shrapnel. Still a bit
of wedding cake [no, not his] on St. Luke's
upper lip. His teeth really something
otherworldly gorgeous to behold
of an evening—Denzel Washington talking
Tyrannosaurus—Luke locks eyes, makes him
dead-to-rights. Kindred. Bullseye. Finale
firework blood vessel bursts, floods
milky sclera. Nearly molten—*Rex*.

LATERAL DRIFT

When Suleyman rode forth—the second Suleyman, mind you—the magnificent,
this latter Suleyman—to lead his Janissaries in battle against the beasts
that had taken for their consort the pliant-thighed
Constantinople, in that moment at front of the conquering
wedge, scimitar aloft, riding on toe-tips high
in jade stirrups Kveldulfur struck... a blank. As for the rest
a bit fuzzy on details, as it was then mid 1500
and over centuries he'd taken several sharp knocks to the jewel-
encrusted skull; the halberd of an unruly Yemeni, the stout tart
he'd sampled in Herzegovina, and at Thessaly for his lurid snicker
that wonderfully surpassed all prior snickers of surpassing wonder.

VERTICAL SHIFT

The number of hotels commendable on the High Atlas dwindles
from none to slightly fewer... the Romans appropriated several good ideas

from the Sammites... irrigation and gyrfalcons—and so did Kubla Khan
in Mongolia, our Mongolia, this ancient tradition of Steppe

boundaries marked with boundary stones and gauntlets. The Khans
only, Genghis particularly with Golden Eagles [more burnished copper]

and with aforementioned gyrfalcons, members of the royal family,
partners, hunted as do the Kazakhs—by this is meant the Berkutchi

riding their stunted ponies—shaggy sand-wolves dreaming
in dust and sun how ridden thermal must feel cradle

to rock-hidden foxes, then muzzles clamped shut
in talons, by talons—a dry and platinum vise.

THE NEW ORTHODOXY

Wherefore Kveldulfur by overturning St. Luke's recycling bins
scattering sundry recyclables well-sorted and poorly, marked

as his territory backyard raw milk bunkers, vats of artisanal
sauerkraut, taxed a bounty upon Luke's hand-stained

custom mobile chicken coop, now empty
but for small fragments of shell therein—apparently German

Spitzhauben—also to the skewbald lie put paid
the palsied claim that dressed in shade, riding

a black charger—a Friesian, or poorly groomed
Hanoverian: it can be difficult to sort Dutch

warmbloods, was the Lord in the form
of a tower. In fact at that time Kveldulfur's hack

a variegated gray, though her gait was high and astounding
her dappling. On their thighs he had marked both village boys

with his quirt and given supple unguent for anointing. Not,
as is sometimes said in more envious circles of islanders,

salve from bacterial drool of the displaced
Komodo Dragons that dwelt beneath City's centerparts

in a mineshaft well East of the airport,
or anything vaguely viral. The dragons,

to their credit, rarely stirred, but one eye of each
was perpetually slitted in vigilance lest the laws of nature

or of traffic should be defiled, as the boys
were said to have been, if one could be said to be defiled

by—all in good fun—a brief but urgent spanking. He'd spanked them
platonically, for the love of God, as he might have spanked,

for Christ's sake, a close friend. Or a staked goat
on which Komodo Dragons are notoriously hard.

SORCHA'S REVELATION

As if actually legit in anticipation finally she melts
the silver coin. Again the tattered paperback
lifted from The Last Bookstore on South Spring.

Mastodon-Schmastodon, no fisheye lens, her fingers
fine enough to thread needles through howevermany angels
fit somethingsomething heads of howevermany pins.

Derringer's grips sport mother-of-pearl inlay, tidy
last minute sniper's bid, her sister's gift, on eBay. Breaks clay
at last room's fabric taut with quiet. Kiss the lost wax

a lingering goodbye against the wall, hard, copped feel
wrapped in cloth, then faint residue, then nothing, then
less, only two lightly lumpen globes at rest

on grape leaf with spider's web with dust with dry leaves
for sail set adrift on what stream returned from what gutter
turned back, what hard iron grate as evening fell

and lava poured over. Lovers forever clutched in ash
enact their own memorials. What you can see of it
is what you get. The greater part's inferred—this time

she consults the lesser coin of zinc
and brass, the horizon's blade, the graven pathways
of sleepless brain as she traipses concrete aisle.

part four

[*Oh, it is awful when you want to talk and can't.*]

—Guy Endore, *The Werewolf of Paris*

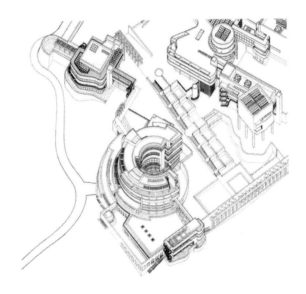

THE RETURN TO FORM

Sun that once peached the frayed harbor
of her fire-peached hips now pales in his throat,
still as any cloister. Sorcha's divulgence, a congenial grin

grown among the chorus. Why now caduceus
risen from the floor of the Villa arboretum?
More gravel to rattle his throat's blank pail.

More. We need more cow bell. Hydrangea bright
in its eastern window box. Hydrangea dull
in the window box shadow box harbor of the West.

EXT. GETTY VILLA COURTYARD, MALIBU - NIGHT

In tempera and gold on parchment we find four little horses,
an ensemble of seven panels, a misapprehended Laguiole cheese
knife's residual butter, shrapnel of Aplets and Cotlets.

THE EXHIBITION: L.A.'s freeway network, corporate towers,
drawings, photographs, films, animations, oral histories, and
ephemera of the laboratory of metropolis.

Finger dangling, uvular wrist to ceiling, baritone tiara in
brilliant canary, SORCHA vamps among Florentine luminaries.

She stashes a <u>BUNDLE OF FABRIC</u> in an adjacent drawing room,
leaves door ajar, tugs free a tiny discernible slip of twill.

AT PARTY: As usual, Christ's crucifixion hogs the spotlight.

INSERT CARD: *Manuscripts in this exhibition have been
transformed again and again to suit the changing expectations
of their various audiences and owners.*

The DOCENTS:

           ST. LUKE   BUGS

ST. LUKE	BUGS
Saint Lawrence, a deacon	Welcome to my shop!
of Rome's third century,	Let me cut your mop!
handed out Rome's money	Let me shave your crop!
to the needy, was ordered	Don't look so perplexed.
burned alive on a George	Why would you be vexed?
Foreman grill. At the end	Can't you see you're next?
of the day my seminal	Yes. You're next.
lesson. Think about it.	You're sooooooo… Next.

Indicative of an innovative approach to popular subject matter,
"There was darkness over the whole earth."

Twenty-eight leaves and fragments survive.

Makes Sundry Leagues of Profligate Knots

If coach says he missed practice and we all heard it,
then that's that. You heard it seized by the puckered stones
and dragged onto the flags of the courtyard
he'd with a single bound made stand on end as if keening.

Luke ever very loose with his loose-hipped walk
unfairly godly lips which he pursed hither and yon to close effect.

If he can't practice then he can't practice. If he's hurt
he's hurt. It's as simple as that. It isn't about that.
When you come into the arena, and you see him play,
you see him play, don't you?

Just a bauble. Just a bauble: a bauble! A pendant bauble.
It hung between her classic breasts. She can finally take off
the tags. Having thumbs doesn't make folding
fitted sheets any easier. There are no returns

excepting St. Luke of the Icons, reprised! Kveldulfur
had never reckoned to have Luke so near
among the bandits and baronets, the board
members and donors.

Dux Bellorum

1.

An insect on its stalk of wildrye the tram
crawls toward travertine pavilions. Fossil-spatter. Traveling

collections. Kveldulfur through his narrow window
notes nothing untoward about the Getty garden, despite the out-of-measure

hissy fit pitched, as it were, the line drawn
in glass bead sand, glass spears unfewtered

and all-to-brast as they had been, between
Sirs Richard Meier and Robert Irwin.

2.

To pinpoint accurately who is Madam Mim and who is Merlin
quite impossible, although as it happens at Buckingham

the Queen still retains her official Champion, a code extended
to wherever Saints conduct a bit of side business with beasts,

give aid to a cornered hare or bleating
crippled lamb. The duel's outcome

irrelevant in terms of violence done by the, or to the, wafer-thin delicious
unleavened holy person of the beatified. Otherwise peaceable beings

living ordinary lives, whatever their appetites,
humankind has always flung headlong at one another, singly

and in hordes, with prim violence or extreme politesse,
wielding handsomely crafted axes, oil-tempered swords

and profit margins, great digital fists. But when he thinks
about big inventions, he thinks about plastic

and he thinks about *denim*, and not in that order.
Know what Eric Estrada was wearing when he invented

the magical interwebs? Blue jeans. Probably Brittania
or Jordache, the imprint of the era. Jordache

actually a beautiful word to ride the lunge-sculpted ass
of a motorcycle cop, a king, or despot-inventor.

3.

And that's all she wrote vis-à-vis the house that Jack built.
For all his hero's shoulder, Luke could hardly whip an épée

to raise a welt, yet that suffices in the end as enough, or almost,
to relegate longing to another age. Life was beautiful then, poxy

and palsy-ridden under waxy sun, blurred by ash
from the corpse-fires. Perhaps inevitable, the nobler version

sans weeping putrefaction and corresponding red stripe
leading the army of affliction straight to the heart

of the drama. Ritual of infection not to be confused
with beauty or the patina of civility.

4.

The whole affair a bald-face bangle of chartreuse
Bakelite [moss green, mossy green] more blue—viridian
Bakelite every patron blurs through window of Lavenderia.
A little bit of fabric softener, of a summer's night,
as it were, carries a very long way, more than a dryer sheet

in dry wind, as she had been. Every day against its scaffolding
of things early and late she'd absconded with all collected
linen, an airy contraband. Every day the chute gate
popped and if the bull weren't that dastard Tony Danza
begat by famed dervish Hotlips Houlihan

he would have ridden under scalpeled sun all the way
to horn before hard-packed earth. Behold
the Monarch on its pin. Behold *The Beast*

mid-air. One-by-one his feet re-touch
the ground. Count them in transition. Count
a boomerang to hand.

5.

St. Luke, as those in the know happen to know, always had an 'in'
or an ace in the hole or escape hatch behind a trick panel
in the library. Cool Hand Luke in the billiards room with a sugar cube,

a sprig of mint. Swift Hand Luke with a parasol, slim
sword therein. And Sorcha, among the first to alight
on carmine, resplendent in vintage Valentino. 15-Love,

Kveldulfur severed beyond reckoning the soiree
of St. Luke's ascent, Sorcha's hand firmly grasped

in his, when rat-to-the-tat, A-to-the-muthafucking-K,
one fat brawny collup of luscious flesh Kveldulfur

sampled from taut hip flexor of St. Luke, quad muscled
as a Williams sister's, ruined Luke's shawl-necked

Brioni tux, for which he was rat-a-tat genuinely
sore aggrieved, tat.

THE TEMPERATURE AT WHICH THINGS MELT

Something shifts him. Three chambers
short a full house heart under fiddle-back
chasuble his back riddled with keloids
leather cuts or hot tallow
down every hard mathematical wall
to the value of five nines a liturgy
in braille. Press him inside shut all doors
under gothic arch then we'll see widow's
peak dialed to high. Then we'll see
what can only be mechanical—pictured only
to illustrate interior quality also this
fabulous Doric pedestal disguised
as body of carbon fiber arrow
distorted en route to fix noon disc
on its pin. What doesn't warp
mid-flight? Consider ink-sleeved scream
of whitelocked double-double
machine: Ball don't lie! As it turns
out, in double-blind of all things
equal, ball don't. Nor for the moment
does that hunger for some other
civilization, the planks of which
have been ripped away, engravings
showing half one thing, half another,
audience crossing and uncrossing
drycleaning tickets, staring at wine spots
on the cyc, toes of fresh kicks
at the charity stripe, the height
of the oak-planked platform, quilted
gambeson of skin, cross-hatched
plate, the foam finger number one
raised at last to storied rafters.

GLOSSY FULL PAGE LAYOUT IN THE DRAWING ROOM

If not near enough to touch
then some essential composition

dispatched in force [On him: embroidered
astrakhan cape; ostrich plume] with orders

to consummate derangement until
no sense can be made of the tumble

of her crepon georgette dress. [On him:
Thom Browne houndstooth

suit, double-breasted caribou overcoat,
John Brown's beard]. Then lying loose

elements at wing wrong-bent
in all directions how encumbered

by this idea it is possible to feel
wrapped in vintage white dress

released this season in vintage
off-white—light breaches it

as it does the gnat poised mid-flight
in amber; the waferesque

Van Cleef & Arpels watch beneath
the band of which the pulse has worn

a little thin. The art of improvisation
is a violent act. He became cutthroat,

gyred, cut current and current knit
behind, an usher. Nictitate. Nictitate,

the lid of the hound settled
on otter's eyerim and otter knifed

sharp wake after. Emissary nerve
affixes, then meteor catches with

her emissary breath. He collapses
beating form into a single grain

of corn and falls into a field
of falling ears, golden stalks,

golden silks, assembled field
draped with cavalcade

of nonchalance, the silent smirk
of virtuosity [season followed

season as back handspring
follows terminal flirt

of Queen's pawn opening] downturned.
She trod the air above the ground

and took the row, a half-pound plow,
barred, leggy, ravenous became

a bantam hen. One bantam foot
clawed black earth over him. Her dirk-

blade beak engaged blank drapes
across the moon. Near—he thought—

certain death, desire stole
his kernelled breath. Desire

[at last the truly PEERLESS
blank] pinioned him. He lay

paralyzed, arable, at last all of his own
making, an offering.

ASTRAL BODY: FULL PANEL BUS ADVERT FITTED WITH SPECIAL GUIDES

In asymmetrical Powder Blue
Burberry trench, the once
not future sorceress slouches
canvas-belted with studded clutch.
Image trembles, idling. Traffic's locked.
Kveldulfur, dream doppelgänger, decamps
bronze Benz, polishes exhaust smut
from model's fringe, but reaches *through*
simulacrum as if searching pond's depths
for vanished key ring, tumbles
forward into hair and makeup suite,
its stupefying pool of tungsten
globes dialed to only setting: *obliterate.*
Post-barrettes, pre-gels-and-mousse,
pre-lining pens, 5 a.m. in tufted vinyl
stylist's seat an actual real live
woman—renown for uncommon
perspicacity, obduration
under pressure, redoubtable
intellect—yawns, masks sweet-sour
morning breath with triplet sticks
of Trident, braces for first airbrush
onslaught, today's assigned
identity. She has her own
[mind]name—her own—it's not,
never was, Hermione.

A SONG OF SIXPENCE

Where now empire of silent screen, empire waist, the scene
in which entire symphony hangs on Sorcha's wrist? How long
does *that* take to learn? Having seared for the umpteenth time

the roof of her mouth—one whole life, at least. A lifetime
of cutting across the bias, sorting funny little fluids
into somber glass phials. All that footage far

too grainy to detect frame
of final reveal. Sorcha resolved
to steal a march

on him and get full shut of it. Smite him upside
the kisser   with that worn reliable standby   Olympian

bolt   then she would have
her satisfaction of him her satisfaction
of all of it. Stitched plaster corset
with knitted bone. Why not
masterhand scrimshaw
on her own exposed
manubrium? That taste
                  for raw

her own desire. Own it :: she owns it :: her own eye teeth
filed just as nice as pointy pie. What's that old philosophical saw

                  every breath takes in
                  so many molecules
                  of Caesar's last, along
                  with pure mélange
                  of everything else
                  uniformly mixed?

All of his substances   already contained in her
she had translated him   was already translated
from her original and   never more squarely
herself

her own roiling composite marine layer fogbank
of hairs/oils/mammal residues/well-deep warm pink
lungs, her very own whole secreting self that miracle
bellow first real breath, her own breath, of next life
a many very great many decomposing—from soil
first wild green shoot—[miracles] of her own.

The Final Scene

No ravishing red-gold Jessica Chastain alabaster
in summer dress caprices family reunion beach. Remodel.
The vanished Ambassador stands in solidarity
with Chavez Ravine. Remodel. Beside a quarter scale
replica of the Watts Towers, remodeled now, revived
in spirit of the archival, the irrepressibly horsey
midcentury Kennedy teeth. Now that's chalet chic,
postcard ski-hill vixen. That's peacock-feathered ceiling
writ complete. Now remodeled with Mercator Projection
printed cape. Now re-branded as Assassin's Honeymoon
Suite. Now with more certainty let us speak not more
of that particular Maxfield Parrish print, that Osborne
& Little flocked damask wallpaper scepter of welded roses,
for ages 8-88, by Mattel, no longer available. Them was
in olden times, Will Munny. Olden ways. Back when
he was sinful. He ain't like that no more. Everyone left
the bar—remodel: none left the bar alive
but the biographer, a near-sighted liar.

RESONANCE CASCADE

A parasol exposed, bright umbrella
unshut indoors, Kveldulfur

stepped from the room, more than naked
completely flensed. The court's hot breathing

scalded him with hot collective
breath. Upon two feet he stood

again and spun upon the ball
of one—at his spine-knobs gasps

from gallery's depths. The steward wrung his vase
of long-stemmed hands. Courtesans blushed

a blooming hedge, but one leaned forward—
he loved her; in the first place

why had he transformed into a man? Kveldulfur,
although each step a gale against

absence of integument, strode to her, took
in both of his raw palms the whole of her

small head, worried in his teeth her
Antarctic prow. With her own fine teeth

she tussled the bald process of his chin.
Her hair, the fine downy at her temples

damp and russet under thumbs.   [Luke eclipsed cracked
Licorice and veneer. Pared nails   door. GARMENT needed tabs
                                        kept and Luke nothing
so close to the quick. Chrome prince   but time time time time time.
if you could only stay   As for the rest, castoff pooled
                                        slough in era of waste
all night. Chrome prince   not want not, let it not be said
I slept but never rested.   that Luke was anything less
                                        than an ardent, although
I have only done   amateur, taxidermist.]
as you might

have, in fact, quite
did, to be who you thought

you needed. Leave go. Are we all
not much of a muchness?

Chrome Prince, what's
to forgive?

THE MILD PERCUSSIVE

Look at it from the top. The crane shot. The vast hydraulic
intrudes—this is the gaze he's talking
of the observer, the fished-for wire hanger

uncoiled and foxed, Extreme Close-Up. You are the oil
in the elbow-piston that would not lock
or unlock, only function. As for your sweater,

you should take it off.
Since flayed now ruined
for normal love I only
want it if it burns
me. Slather me
with Silvadene but
don't   don't touch
because it   all

does.

       Brave Gallardo, Fusileer, will you remember this the way I will?

Drawn Toledo.   Dragon Roll at Umi.   Mother-of-pearl.   Flemish charge.

    /   \

    Sorcha pearlish shoots him through his pearlish heart

  \   /

                           Okay. Wait - it's
                           okay. He actually
                           prefers a touch of shell
                           in his over-easy. Hold
                           on. Hold up. Hold
                           me. Together, let's
                           just take this shape
                           and hold it until
                           last vibrations
                           stop.

[she pats his shoulder with derringer barrel, all in say, transubstantiation, like.
CUT: actors back to 1, please, back to 1 please: the boom was in the shot.]

The Reality Body Between Takes

As for his seat, he had been so glued
to it, then broadening sweet glaze
of Jolly Rancher disambiguating

across the dash of the Range Rover
as sun leapt high then came too near
then strawberry fields forever, or at least

from here to that plate mail visor
with stunningly embossed beaver. Stunning of course
in terms of craftsmanship, though the glare

obscures cunning surface of the mask
blurred by blast of very own radiant machine
berserked unto abstraction. All aboard

and bon courage. Too many clothes
pins stegosaur his spine. Thumbs up
for endorphins but bales upon bales

of luxurious chiffons make getting past
the guards in this get up a bit of a dilem—that is,
a perfect diadem—that is, a question: if he should leap

will this body return to lineage of one renter
born to another, return anchored
to catwalk, to wing, to voice, cantilever

-ed braid? He'd always thought
his one true impulse to outlast
but is already heavy bored

with that, the simple matter
of existence, the same participatory cannibal
as when you took your pamphlet

at the door. Does it not change
as it enters the ear? It does
but he does not. Until now

not enough. Had thought himself
finally beyond surprise. Bless her
finger bless the trigger.

FREQUENTLY A SHORTNESS OF BREATH

A thready, rapid pulse. The aforementioned scent
of fabric softener now carries even farther
than once-just-a-slip-of-dryer-sheet-in-dry-wind

as she had, as we all have been, each day pinned
against its scaffolding of things, coddled slights
and rusted hinges. Previously, architects multiplied

such panels as granted great reverses
and it was so. Ultimately how necessary
to incinerate magnesium buttresses,

The Forum's magnesium hull. Nil by mouth
and aught else though a fair case made either way,
resounding judgments handed down of categorical

double-outlawry for excellent good cancelling
though it is known such a ruling cannot delete
burned-in stamp, only deepen it. Sorcha no longer

turned on end and divided nor subject to such
division nor anyone ever on this island
capable of such convincing. Once again,

scalpel fragments sun. She collects
fragments one-by-one, now counts
the cost, the four-fold cramp as if

she had been stabbed deeply into
still water. A heavy branch released   leaps
after having long been held under.

part five

[And still she was on that point of dissolving and could not dissolve.]

—Guy Endore, The Werewolf of Paris

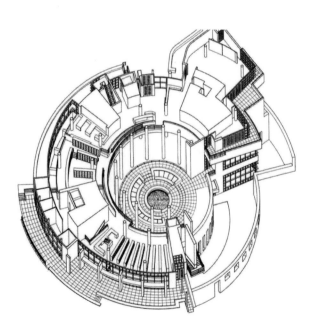

EXT. MULLHOLLAND DRIVE AND TOPANGA CANYON - WEEKS LATER - NIGHT

Wilderness, L.A. County. WIND rakes brush, desiccated oak. City
glows over the rise. Down the draw, a wildcat SCREAMS. Community
sleeps the sleep of having a nationally-ranked school system.

THE BEAST trots onto a private full-sized tennis court lit by
Mercury Vapor lamps. From house the TRICKLE of infinity pool.

This Beast is lighter of frame. Darker of eye. Around her, scent
streams eddy byways like dry pigments spilled into a water vat.

FLARE of headlights. Car doors SLAM. CHILDREN'S VOICES.

The Beast skirts chain link, recedes into landscaped treeline.

EXT. GRIFFITH OBSERVATORY - HOURS LATER

Behold The Beast suspended between valences, front legs planted
on concrete pressed with the mask of stonework terraces.

BELOW:

Arclight Cinema floodlamps wash the sky with discs. Flashing
sirens sporadically tickle the grid, which resembles a vast
complex of bicycle rims spinning imperceptibly on electric axes.

As if conjured, one luminous tree sprouts near Olympic and
Normandie, matures in an instant, bears one prodigious fruit…

…that RUPTURES, peels, presents a glossy pit, which CRACKS OPEN
to reveal A ROOM in which ST. CATHERINE extends swan wings from
cellophane kimono sleeves, reclines to drowse upon the wheel.

Space collapses, as usual. The Beast steps through…

INT. ROOM INSIDE THE SEED - CONTINUOUS

Birch-plank walls glazed in amber lacquers, vitreous enamels.

Head ducked, Catherine's footman kneels on tufted ottoman, a
rolled parchment offered on his raised palms. The Beast reads:

*"Your indiscreetly broadcast revelation that we all harbor
cells from other beings in these our presumed [HA!] hallowed
fortresses violates all understanding of former treatied
agreement. Consider this notification of egregious breach of
covenant. Consider covenant now null. Consider us ill pleased.
We persist, recused."*

By simple force of will, Catherine molts to the wrists, reveals
exposed roots that once drew nourishment to her beech-wood crown,
but now tap a leached field pocked by moles, violated by kine.

The room shudders, scales over like a pangolin, reduces, a
balloon banishing all helium. First seed then tree then light
extinguishes. Fine dust falls toward curb, never reaches it.

EXT. GRIFFITH OBSERVATORY - CONTINUOUS

C.U. Behold The Beast as revenant, first eye-blink as permanent
resident. Black-lined lips lift as if by puppet-strings.

Corduroy abrades corduroy in the gallery of her throat. Attendant
temblor shakes doors off once locked furnaces, and yet…

She will not *howl*. Will not.

She means to SPEAK.

THE DAY OF OUR WEDDING IS EVERY DAY

K nock, knock: eight yellow raspberries
in straight strong doses. That old joke.
How little against which to struggle
or resist, now that I am, perforce,
in on it. Hove there a dusky barge? Three
black-stoled queens crowned in gold?
No barge no queens only bright vast hull
forever in one place   then clothed the sky
and covered all.

                                        When you fell

through broad air how many
voices spoke at once? Garrote me

                        with barbed wire how we practiced
                        once with floss   when through snow you fell

kept falling from union you fell
with some broken
future you fell you
populate me I populate

                        this   finally the only kindness
                        capable of proper undoing
                        so I lean into it kiss me
                                        kiss me with

your jaws kiss me with your eyeteeth
ivories   don't kiss me

with your lips that bullet   you fell
mad flurry

                                blizzard

of light   hush   susurration of slight

hush

FADE TO WHITE.

NOTES

The concept, intention, and occasion of *The Getty Fiend* is a distorted
retelling of Marie Du France's *le lai du Bisclavret*, composted and
compounded with Guy Endore's gothic horror pulp novel, *The Werewolf
of Paris*, with the notable exception of featuring as its initial protagonist
a storied Icelandic shapechanger from the Bronze Age—all set in
contemporary Los Angeles

In addition to the sources and inspirations noted above, some of the
poems in this book are in conversation with, quote, paraphrase, disfigure,
or appropriate ideas or phrases from Djuna Barnes, John Berryman, Walt
Disney, Wolfram von Eschenbach, Geoffrey of Monmouth, Jean Genet,
Robert Graves, Allen Iverson, A.O.H. Jarman, Arthur Krystal, Sir Thomas
Malory, Prince, J. K. Rowling, Montague Summers, Alfred Lord Tennyson,
Sojourner Truth, *The Unforgiven*, Rasheed Wallace, *The Wizard of Oz*, and
Virginia Woolf, as well as various translations of *Egil's Saga*, *The Poetic Edda*,
Hanes Taliesin, *Llyfr Du Caerfyrddin*, *Buile Shuibhne*, and *The Mabinogion*.
Select snippets from a decade of display placards from exhibitions at the
Getty Villa and The J. Paul Getty Center are also embedded in the text.

ACKNOWLEDGMENTS

Versions of some of the poems in this collection have appeared in the following literary journals, and I am deeply grateful to the editors who published them: *Manor House Quarterly*, *Poets.org*, and *Action, Yes*.

I'd also like to thank the people who have generously given of their time, energy, language, and insight to help shape the many iterations of this manuscript into its current form: Brian Blanchfield, Greg Brooker, Teresa Carmody, Michael du Plessis, Lorraine Graham, Joanna Klink, James Meetze, Vanessa Place, Prageeta Sharma, Richard Siken, S.T., Jeanine Webb, and Andrew Wessels.

BIOGRAPHICAL NOTES

Ken White is a co-writer and co-producer of the feature film *Winter in the Blood*, adapted from James Welch's novel of the same name, and co-director and co-writer of the short film *Universal VIP*. He has written or co-written ten feature scripts. His poetry has appeared in *The Boston Review*, *The Tusculum Review*, *Columbia: A Journal of Literature and Art*, *Versal*, *Omniverse*, *Manor House Quarterly*, *Spork*, *Horsethief*, *Poets.org*, and *Action, Yes*, among others. He is the author of the book of poems, *Eidolon* (Peel Press 2013), as well as *Middlemost Constantine* (forthcoming from Spork 2017). White teaches screenwriting at the low-residency MFA at the Institute of American Indian Arts in Santa Fe.

Michael du Plessis is author of the novel *The Memoirs of JonBenet by Kathy Acker* (Les Figues 2017) and the chapbook *Songs Dead Soldiers Sing* (2007) Michael's writing has appeared in journals and periodicals from *THE FANZINE* to *French Forum*.